ANTIQUES AND THEIR VALUES

CHAIRS & COUCHES

COMPILED BY TONY CURTIS

First Published   June 1977
Reprinted   October 1977
Revised Edition   June 1978

Exchange Rate $2 = £1

Original Edition ISBN   0-902921-47-9
Revised Edition ISBN   0-902921-73-8

Copyright Ⓒ Lyle Publications 1977.
Published by Lyle Publications, Glenmayne, Galashiels, Scotland.
Distributed in the U.S.A. by Apollo, 391 South Road, Poughkeepsie, N.Y. 12601.

INTRODUCTION

Congratulations! You now have in your hands an extremely valuable book. It is one of a series specially devised to aid the busy professional dealer in his everyday trading. It will also prove to be of great value to all collectors and those with goods to sell, for it is crammed with illustrations, brief descriptions and valuations of hundreds of antiques.

Every effort has been made to ensure that each specialised volume contains the widest possible variety of goods in its particular category though the greatest emphasis is placed on the middle bracket of trade goods rather than on those once - in - a - lifetime museum pieces whose values are of academic rather than practical interest to the vast majority of dealers and collectors.

This policy has been followed as a direct consequence of requests from dealers who sensibly realise that, no matter how comprehensive their knowledge, there is always a need for reliable, up-to-date reference works for identification and valuation purposes.

When using your Antiques and their Values to assess the worth of goods, please bear in mind that it would be impossible to place upon any item a precise value which would hold good under all circumstances. No antique has an exactly calculable value; its price is always the result of a compromise reached between buyer and seller, and questions of condition, local demand and the business acumen of the parties involved in a sale are all factors which affect the assessment of an object's 'worth' in terms of hard cash.

In the final analysis, however, such factors cancel out when large numbers of sales are taken into account by an experienced valuer, and it is possible to arrive at a surprisingly accurate assessment of current values of antiques; an assessment which may be taken confidently to be a fair indication of the worth of an object and which provides a reliable basis for negotiation.

Throughout this book, objects are grouped under category headings and, to expedite reference, they progress in price order within their own categories. Where the description states 'one of a pair' the value given is that for the pair sold as such.

Printed by Apollo Press, Dominion Way, Worthing, Sussex, England.
Bound by Newdigate Press, Vincent Lane, Dorking, Surrey, England.

CONTENTS

ARM CHAIRS

Mid 19th century bentwood arm chair. $30 £15

Late Victorian elm kitchen chair on turned legs with turned cross stretchers. $40 £20

A stained arm chair with hard seat. $40 £20

Victorian elm smoker's chair with a saddle seat. $50 £25

A Victorian carved oak high back arm chair, with cane back and seat. $50 £25

A fine 19th century stained arm chair, on fluted legs, the seat covered in velour.$50 £25

Elm high ladder-back arm chair with rush seat.
$60 £30

Mahogany bergere arm chair on square tapered legs of Adam design. $60 £30

Regency fruitwood arm chair with reeded rail back and leather seat. $70 £35

Child's Chinese bamboo chair, circa 1880. $80 £40

Mahogany arm chair on cabriole legs. $80 £40

A 19th century mahogany arm chair, on square legs. $80 £40

19th century child's elm commode chair. $80 £40

18th century elm splat back chair. $84 £42

A large late Victorian mahogany open arm chair, with panel back and seat in damask. $90 £45

Victorian elm ladder-back carver chair. $96 £48

A mahogany Art Nouveau arm chair, with tall narrow back, inlaid splat, on square tapering legs. $100 £50

A mahogany and ivory inlaid arm chair on cabriole legs. $100 £50

9

ARM CHAIRS

Edwardian mahogany occasional chair with a pierced back splat and padded seat. $100 £50

Late 18th century country made Chippendale style carver. $100 £50

An oak arm chair with carved panel back and hard-wood seat. $104 £52

A small Orkney wing chair with hardwood seat. $108 £54

Early Victorian mahogany elbow chair on turned legs. $110 £55

A carved oak arm chair of Italian design on shaped supports. $110 £55

A Georgian elm arm chair with pierced splat , on square moulded legs. $120 £60

Early 19th century mahogany framed, sabre leg dining chair. $120 £60

A mahogany arm chair in George III style, the rectangular back with Chinese fret splat. $120 £60

Edwardian mahogany and marquetry inlaid arm chair. $124 £62

William IV period mahogany elbow chair on turned legs. $130 £65

A George III elm arm chair, with pierced splat and a drop in seat. $130 £65

A primitive Welsh farmhouse spinning wheel chair of solid ashwood, circa 1760. $130 £65

Victorian bobbin back elbow chair in mahogany with a drop in seat. $130 £65

Sheraton mahogany arm chair, with spar back, on square tapering legs. $130 £65

Sheraton mahogany arm chair with turned reeded spar back, on square tapered legs. $130 £65

19th century oak caquetoise. $130 £65

One of a pair of 19th century dining chairs of Chippendale design with carved and pierced vase shaped splats, on cabriole legs. $130 £65

11

ARM CHAIRS

A 19th century carved walnut open arm chair, on turnball legs and stretcher with foot rest, the shaped panel back carved with a coat-of-arms. $130 £65

One of a set of five late 19th century oak dining chairs with pierced splats, on square tapering legs $144 £72

A Regency mahogany arm chair, reeded, on sabre legs, the drop in seat in green fringed velvet. $160 £80

One of a pair of Queen Anne style ebonised arm chairs, on cabriole legs, painted with figures. $160 £80

Mahogany elbow chair in mid 18th century style with tapestry work seat. $160 £80

Set of three Regency mahogany dining chairs, with reeded uprights and panelled toprail, on turned legs. $160 £80

One of a pair of Victorian scroll arm chairs on turned legs. $164 £82

19th century Oriental hardwood chair inlaid with bone and ivory $170 £85

Sheraton mahogany arm chair with trellis splat, on square fluted tapering legs, the seat covered in tapestry. $170 £85

12

18th century rush
seated spindle back
arm chair, circa 1760,
39¼in. high. $180 £90

Regency period
ebonised elbow
chair. $180 £90

George III walnut
Captain's chair
with solid walnut
seat, circa 1760.
$184 £92

Early 19th century
Empire style arm
chair with a padded
back and seat. $190 £95

Indian carved teak
arm chair on tur-
ned legs and
stretchers. $190 £95

Sheraton style
mahogany
elbow chair,
circa 1820. $200 £100

One of a pair of 19th
century Chippendale
style mahogany elbow
chairs with loose seats,
on cabriole legs, with
ball and claw feet. $200 £100

George I oak
wainscot chair.
$220 £110

Chippendale period
arm chair of faded
mahogany, 21in.
wide, circa 1780. $230
£115

ARM CHAIRS

One of a set of
four pine chairs,
circa 1900. $240 £120

Regency sabre leg
mahogany elbow
chair with reeded
members. $260 £130

Mahogany Chippendale
elbow chair, circa 1760.
$260
£130

17th century oak
wainscot chair.
$260 £130

Victorian papier mache
arm chair with a cane
seat. $290 £145

Restoration period
walnut caned arm
chair, circa 1680.
$350 £175

One of a pair of Regency
bergere chairs in rose-
wood with reeded sabre
legs. $350 £175

One of a set of eight oak
dining chairs with leather
backs and seats, on spiral
legs and stretchers (2 & 6).
$350 £175

18th century
Dutch marquetry
elbow chair. $360
£180

14

Charles II carved
walnut arm chair.
$360 £180

Chippendale period
mahogany arm chair,
circa 1760. $360 £180

One of a pair of Sheraton
style elbow chairs, in
mahogany, circa 1810.
$370
£185

English carved
oak elbow chair,
circa 1763. $380 £190

Mid Victorian
open arm chair.
$380 £190

One of a pair of fine
Gothic chairs, about
1820-30, 25in. wide.
$400
£200

Late 17th century wal-
nut carver chair with
cane back and seat.
$410 £205

One of a pair of open
arm chairs in
mahogany. $420 £210

One of a set of eight
chairs with cane
backs, on spiral legs
and stretchers. $420
£210

ARM CHAIRS

Late 18th century Hepplewhite japanned arm chair with a cane seat. $420 £210

William IV marquetry carver chair with scroll arms. $420 £210

A giltwood bergere chair, circa 1830. $430 £215

Louis XV beechwood chair on cabriole legs, circa 1750. $430 £215

17th century oak arm chair with a carved back and front rail. $470 £235

Carolean walnut chair, with cane back and seat. $470 £235

Mahogany arm chair by Gillows, circa 1790. $480 £240

One of a pair of Chinese padouk wood elbow chairs. $480 £240

One of a set of eight oak dining chairs, with cane backs and seats, on spiral legs and stretchers. $480 £240

16

An ebonised chair designed by E.W. Godwin, circa 1870. $480 £240

One of a pair of mahogany arm chairs of Chippendale design, with carved top rail and pierced vase shaped splats. $490 £245

One of a pair of late 18th century Continental arm chairs. $530 £265

North Italian walnut chair with Moresque ivory inlay. $550 £275

One of a set of six mahogany dining chairs of Hepplewhite design, with hoop backs and pierced splats, on square tapered legs. $550 £275

East Anglican oak wainscot chair, circa 1700. $550 £275

One of a set of three chairs, with attractive pierced wheatsheaf back splat. $560 £280

One of a set of eight mahogany dining chairs on cabriole legs, the drop in seats covered in velvet, (2 & 6). $540 £270

Mid 17th century upholstered 'X' frame chair. $600 £300

ARM CHAIRS

Set of eight oak dining chairs (2 & 6) with rush seats, by Heale & Sons, circa 1910. $600 £300

17th century heavily carved oak elbow chair. $620 £310

Set of eight dining chairs of Georgian design, on square legs, (2 & 6).$620 £310

17th century oak wainscot chair, inlaid to panel back and broad cresting rail. $640 £320

One of a pair of Menlesham elbow chairs of fruitwood, with figured elm seats and boxwood stringing. $650 £325

One of a pair of Queen Anne walnut chairs with oak slats. $660 £330

One of a set of eight oak chairs, circa 1800. $710 £355

One of a pair of Dutch marquetry open arm chairs.$710 £355

One of a set of six 18th century (2 & 4) spindleback chairs, with rush seats. $720 £360

18

One of a set of eight mahogany dining chairs of Chippendale design, with carved and pierced vase shaped splats, on cabriole legs, with ball and claw feet.$720 £360

A Regency spoon back chair of simulated rosewood having the original brass mounts. $740 £370

One of a set of six mahogany ladder back chairs. $770 £385

One of a set of six late Georgian mahogany dining chairs. $840 £420

One of a set of six William IV dining chairs upholstered in leather. $840 £420

Rare late 17th century walnut framed open arm chair. $860 £430

Late 18th century Chippendale mahogany scroll arm elbow chair. $890 £445

One of a set of six Chippendale ribbon back chairs, circa 1850. $950 £475

George II collapsible mahogany campaign chair, circa 1750. $960 £480

19

ARM CHAIRS

One of a set of six Regency ebonised dining chairs. $960 £480

A fine quality George II red walnut arm chair, with cabriole legs and pad feet, circa 1740. $980 £490

One of a pair of elbow chairs with tapered legs. $1,020 £510

One of a pair of Spanish walnut arm chairs, circa 1700. $1,020 £510

George II American open arm chair in faded honey colour Virginia red walnut, circa 1745. $1,020 £510

James I arm chair of oak and pine. $1,030 £515

One of a set of eight George III mahogany dining chairs with carved and fluted spar backs. $1,040 £520

Georgian cock fighting chair. $1,080 £540

One of a pair of late 18th century mahogany arm chairs with triple pierced splats and needlework seats. $1,080 £540

James I oak
arm chair.
$1,100 £550

One of a set of three
late 18th century
beechwood elbow
chairs with cane
seats. $1,130 £565

A fine 17th century
carved oak wainscot
chair. $1,260 £630

Charles II walnut car-
ved chair, sold with
two standards, circa
1680. $1,260 £630

One of a pair of
late 17th century
carved oak chairs.
             $1,280 £640

One of a set of six
Georgian mahogany
chairs, two carvers
and four singles.
             $1,320 £660

George I walnut veneered
arm chair with cabriole
legs and ball and claw
feet. $1,320 £660

One of a set of four
Regency open arm
chairs with cane seats.
             $1,440 £720

A leather covered,
mahogany master's
chair with intricately
carved arm and back
supports. $1,460 £730

ARM CHAIRS

One of a set of six dark mahogany chairs with serpentine fronts, circa 1850. $1,520 £760

One of a set of four George I mahogany chairs, 4ft.4in. high. $1,580 £790

One of a set of eight (6 & 2) Chippendale style mahogany chairs, circa 1860. $1,620 £810

Charles I oak arm chair. $1,620 £810

One of a set of six Provincial quality Sheraton chairs, circa 1790. $1,680 £840

Late Elizabethan arm chair. $1,780 £890

One of a set of seven Sheraton period mahogany chairs, circa 1780. $1,800 £900

One of a set of four Chinese hardwood chairs inlaid with ivory. $1,800 £900

17th century oak arm chair with scroll carving. $1,800 £900

A Queen Anne japanned arm chair. $1,920 £960

One of a set of eight oak dining chairs, 17th century. $2,020 £1,010

One of a set of eight finely carved 19th century reproduction Chippendale mahogany dining chairs, with scroll feet and cabriole legs. $2,160 £1,080

One of a set of six Sheraton gilt painted and lacquered armed dining chairs with lattice backs. $2,400 £1,200

Elizabethan arm chair with a squab cushion. $2,420 £1,210

One of a set of seven early 19th century simulated bamboo chairs. $2,420 £1,210

One of a pair of 17th century Chinese hardwood hoop backed chairs. $2,640 £1,320

One of a set of ten mahogany arm chairs in the Hepplewhite style, with serpentine fronted seats. $2,750 £1,375

One of a set of eight Regency mahogany chairs with reeded sabre legs. $2,750 £1,375

ARM CHAIRS

18th century Indian ivory veneered chair of early Georgian style. $2,750 £1,375

Late Elizabethan carved and inlaid walnut arm chair. $2,750 £1,375

One of a set of eight mahogany dining arm chairs of Queen Anne design, with solid shaped splats, on cabriole legs. $2,860 £1.430

One of a set of eight Regency black and gilt elbow chairs. $2,860 £1,430

Unusual set of six English mahogany arm chairs, circa 1800. $3,300 £1,650

One of a set of six early 19th century mahogany framed elbow chairs, with caned seats and backs. $3,300 £1,650

James I inlaid and carved oak arm chair. $3,410 £1.705

One of a set of twelve Chippendale mahogany dining chairs. $3,520 £1,760

Late Elizabethan oak arm chair with a canvas and cord seat. $3,630 £1,815

One of a set of twelve Hepplewhite style chairs with shield backs. $3,630 £1,815

One of a pair of Charles I oak arm chairs. $4,000 £2,000

One of a set of eight, two carvers, six singles, Dutch marquetry dining chairs. $4,000 £2,000

One of a set of nine harlequin 18th century mahogany dining chairs. $4,200 £2,100

One of a pair of mahogany elbow chairs of French Hepplewhite design. $5,000 £2,500

Arm chair from a set of twelve George II mahogany dining chairs. $12,000 £6,000

One of a set of eight George III mahogany shield back arm chairs with reeded and carved splats, on square tapering legs. $12,200 £6,100

One of a set of four Gothic revival chairs. $13,200 £6,600

A chair by Charles Rennie Mackintosh, made for the owner of The Willow Tea Rooms, Glasgow. $20,000 £10,000

CORNER CHAIRS

An ebonised corner chair, the seat covered in green velour. $50 £25

Edwardian mahogany tub chair on turned legs. $70 £35

A mahogany corner chair with two carved and pierced splats, on turned legs, with rush seat. $80 £40

George III elm corner chair. $90 £45

Edwardian inlaid mahogany corner chair on turned legs with stretchers. $100 £50

Unusual Edwardian inlaid mahogany corner chair. $100 £50

Edwardian mahogany elbow chair with a pierced back splat and cabriole legs. $100 £50

William IV mahogany and caned bobbin backed corner elbow chair. $104 £52

Edwardian corner chair decorated in the Chinese style. $110 £55

A carved oak corner
chair with animal
head terminals. $120 £60

18th century elm
wood corner chair
with turned
supports. $190 £95

A fine George II
oak corner arm
chair, circa 1750.
$240 £120

Early 19th century
turned wood chair,
circa 1820. $260 £130

Late 18th century Dutch
marquetry corner chair
on cabriole legs with
paw feet. $430 £215

One of a pair of
oak throne chairs,
original condition.
$540 £270

Queen Anne period
walnut corner chair.
$540 £270

Small George II Cuban
mahogany corner chair
with well carved open
splats and fluted legs,
circa 1755. $830 £415

Early 18th century
walnut corner chair,
George I about 1727,
31 in. wide. $1,680 £840

27

DAY BEDS

Early Victorian day bed with loose cushion. $160 £80

Upholstered day bed with circle end and half back, 156cm. long. $260 £130

Military convertible officer's chair-bed in iron and brass, circa 1840-60. $360 £180

An early oak day bed, 66in. long, 22in. wide. $590 £29

Good quality Victorian day bed upholstered in gold velvet. $720 £360

William and Mary walnut day bed, with attractively shaped back and legs. $720 £360

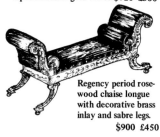

Regency period rose-wood chaise longue with decorative brass inlay and sabre legs. $900 £450

Russian chaise longue in amboyna with gilded carving. $12,000 £6,000

George III elm
kitchen chair
with a hard seat.
$20 £10

19th century
bentwood chair.
$20 £10

Edwardian inlaid
mahogany dining
chair. $24 £12

Victorian child's
chair in ash.$24 £12

19th century mahogany
dining chair with pierced
vase shaped splat.$30 £15

19th century child's
chair in elm. $30 £15

19th century beech-
wood child's chair
with caned seat. $30 £15

Victorian carved
oak spinning chair.
$40 £20

Victorian cast iron cir-
cular verandah chair
with acanthus leaf back. $44
£22

DINING CHAIRS

Late 18th century oak dining chair. $48 £24

.Mahogany chair with solid splat and upholstered seat, on cabriole legs. $52 £26

One of a pair of Thonet bentwood children's chairs with the original upholstery, circa 1870. $56 £28

Mahogany chair with pierced ladder back. $56 £28

19th century Oriental teak folding chair, profusely inlaid with bone and ivory. $60 £30

One of a pair of white and green painted chairs of Louis XVI design. $60 £30

One of two stained chairs of Cromwellian design with leather panel backs and seats. $64 £32

One of a set of four stained dining chairs on cabriole legs. $68 £34

One of a set of four Edwardian beech ladder back chairs. $68 £3

Victorian papier mache chair on cabriole legs with mother-of-pearl inlay and cane seat. $84 £42

Regency artist's chair of simulated bamboo.
$84 £42

One of a pair of Edwardian mahogany bedroom chairs.
$84 £42

Continental Regency style occasional chair.
$84 £42

A mahogany spinning chair, decorated with flowers. $84 £42

One of a pair of Victorian carved oak chairs. $88 £44

One of a pair of George III mahogany spar back dining chairs. $88 £44

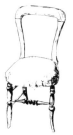

One of a set of four Victorian beechwood kitchen chairs. $90 £45

One of a set of six Edwardian mahogany dining chairs with turned legs and padded backs. $90 £45

31

DINING CHAIRS

One of a set of three Edwardian chairs with serpentine toprails and medallion inlaid splats. $100 £50

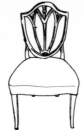

One of two Hepplewhite style mahogany shield back chairs. $100 £50

One of a set of four Victorian flat splat kitchen chairs. $100 £50

One of a pair of George III mahogany dining chairs with pierced splats. $100 £50

One of a pair of 19th century Oriental dining chairs. $110 £55

One of a set of four Victorian mahogany chairs. $110 £55

Edwardian Sheraton style chair of mahogany with boxwood stringing, 26½in. high. $110 £55

One of a set of four late Victorian, Queen Anne style beechwood chairs with drop in seats and cabriole legs. $110 £55

One of a pair of giltwood bedroom chairs on turned legs, with cane seats. $110 £55

A rare spindle back ash-wood miniature chair with a rush seat, circa 1790, 17in. high. $110 £55

One of a set of six carved mahogany Edwardian chairs on turned legs. $110 £55

One of a set of three late 19th century dining chairs with pierced splats. $110 £55

One of a set of four Victorian beech-wood chairs with upholstered seats. $110 £55

One of a set of four Edwardian carved walnut chairs with padded backs. $110 £55

19th century maho-gany correction chair. $120 £60

One of a pair of bamboo bedroom chairs. $120 £60

One of a set of five late 19th century mahogany chairs on turned legs. $120 £60

One of a set of four Victorian mahogany chairs on turned and fluted legs. $120 £60

DINING CHAIRS

An early 19th century Continental spinning wheel chair, with bobbin back splats. $130 £65

One of a pair of carved walnut seats of French design, on turned and fluted legs. $130 £65

Queen Anne single oak chair in original condition, 39in. high, circa 1705. $140 £7

One of a set of four late 19th century walnut chairs in the French style. $144 £72

19th century marquetry dining chair. $144 £72

18th century French oak bow seated chair. $144 £7

One of a pair of Louis XVI style carved walnut chairs, on turned and fluted legs. $144 £72

One of a set of three Victorian walnut chairs, with carved and pierced splats, on cabriole legs. $144 £72

One of three George III mahogany dining chairs. $144 £72

One of a set of six 20th century Queen Anne style dining chairs on cabriole legs, with cane backs. $160 £80

Cast iron conservatory chair, the three legs entwined with ribbons of iron, on leaf feet.$160 £80

One of a pair of Victorian gossip chairs, with carved and pierced splats, ornate toprails and flower design tapestry type seats. $160 £80

A ship's chair on original dark green finish, a Nelson sea battle scene painted on the back rest. $160 £80

One of a set of four late 19th century mahogany dining chairs. $160 £80

One of a set of four rosewood dining chairs on octagonal legs. $170 £85

Early 19th century Dutch marquetry chair with sabre legs. $180 £90

One of a set of four Edwardian inlaid mahogany dining chairs. $180 £90

One of a pair of George III mahogany dining chairs, the carved toprails and open splats with flowers and acanthus leaves, on square legs and stretchers. $180 £90

35

DINING CHAIRS

One of a set of four rosewood dining chairs with carved ball and turnball designs. $190 £95

One of a set of four early 19th century simulated bamboo chairs with cane seats. $190 £95

Late 18th century Hepplewhite mahogany dining chair. $200 £100

One of a set of four Victorian mahogany turned leg chairs with Trafalgar seats. $200 £100

Queen Anne walnut side chair with pad feet, circa 1710. $200 £100

One of a set of four Victorian mahogany circle back dining chairs with buttoned leather seats, on turned legs. $200 £100

One of a pair of Provincial oak chairs, about 1880, 36in. high. $200 £100

One of a set of four Georgian mahogany dining chairs. $220 £110

One of a set of four early Victorian bar back chairs in mahogany with turned legs. $220 £110

One of a pair of Hepplewhite chairs. $230 £115

One of a set of nine oak spoon back chairs on turned legs. $230 £115

One of a set of four mahogany drawing room chairs with shield shaped backs, carved and pierced splats, on cabriole legs. $230 £115

One of a set of six Victorian dining chairs on turned legs, the seats covered in crimson damask covers. $240 £120

Chippendale mahogany chair, carved top rail. $240 £120

A late 17th century walnut chair. $250 £125

One of a set of four Edwardian mahogany dining chairs inlaid with boxwood. $260 £130

Queen Anne oak dining chair of good colour. $260 £130

One of a set of six ebonised side chairs with a caned seat, turned legs and arched splats in the arched back. $260 £130

DINING CHAIRS

Queen Anne style walnut chair with ladder back. $280 £140

Single 17th century oak chair. $280 £140

One of a set of four 18th century elm ladder back chairs with rush seats. $290 £14(

Early 18th century padouk wood chair with an embossed leather seat and back. $290 £145

One of a set of five oak chairs of medium colour, circa 1800. $300 £150

19th century carved oak cockfighting chair with heraldic lions holding a shield with initials C.R. $300 £150

One of a set of four mid 19th century walnut framed dining chairs with padded backs and overstuffed seats. $300 £150

One of a set of four 19th century reeded mahogany chairs on sabre legs. $300 £150

One of a set of four early 19th century French carved walnut chairs on cabriole legs. $310 £155

One of a set of six mahogany dining chairs with pierced splats, on square legs and stretchers. $320 £160

One of a set of five Victorian rosewood dining chairs. $320 £160

A fine example of a 17th century oak chair. $320 £160

One of a set of six Victorian mahogany dining chairs. $340 £170

Charles II walnut high back chair. $340 £170

One of a set of four Victorian rosewood dining chairs on cabriole legs, the seats covered in rep. $360 £180

Walnut high back chair elaborately carved, circa 1675. $360 £180

Queen Anne wall chair with central splat. $360 £180

Unusual laminated Regency period dining chair. $370 £185

DINING CHAIRS

One of a set of five Sheraton mahogany dining chairs with carved and fluted spar backs. $380 £190

One of a set of ten Hepplewhite design mahogany dining chairs with shield backs. $380 £190

One of a set of six mahogany dining chairs with pierced splats and drop in seats. $380 £190

A handsome oak Yorkshire chair, circa 1650. $380 £190

One of a set of three 19th century marquetry dining chairs. $380 £190

One of a set of four Regency rosewood dining chairs, with fluted toprails and brass mounts to splats, on sabre legs. $390 £1

One of a set of six Yorkshire chairs with rush seats, 34in. high, circa 1840. $420 £210

One of a set of six Victorian carved oak dining chairs with upholstered back and seat. $420 £210

One of a set of four Victorian walnut chairs. $420 £210

One of a fine pair of cockfighting chairs. $430 £215

A 17th century oak chair with carved back support. $430 £215

Queen Anne walnut single chair with plain shaped splat back, front cabriole legs, carved with foliage. $460 £230

One of a set of six Victorian walnut dining chairs. $460 £230

One of a pair of 17th century upholstered oak standard chairs. $470 £235

One of a pair of 17th century oak standard chairs. $470 £235

One of a set of four Victorian walnut salon chairs. $480 £240

One of a set of six Victorian rosewood chairs, on turned and fluted supports. $500 £250

One of a set of six Regency simulated rosewood dining chairs with sabre front legs and drop in seat. $510 £255

41

DINING CHAIRS

Early 17th century
Derbyshire chair.
$530 £265

One of a set of six
George III maho-
gany dining chairs.
$530 £265

One of a set of four
19th century Dutch
marquetry chairs. $55█
£27.

One of a set of six
spindle back dining
chairs, circa 1800.
$550 £275

One of a set of six
19th century maho-
gany sabre leg chairs.
$550 £275

One of a set of six elm
framed chairs, with
green upholstered
seats, circa 1800. $580
£290

One of a set of six light
mahogany chairs, circa
1870. $590 £295

One of a set of seven
Regency period chairs
in simulated rosewood,
circa 1830. $590 £295

One of a set of six
wavy ladder back
chairs with rush
seats. $600 £300

DINING CHAIRS

William and Mary chair in walnut, of superb quality and proportions 45in. high, circa 1690.
$600 £300

One of a set of six early 19th century rosewood chairs.
$600 £300

One of a set of six Victorian carved walnut chairs.
$620 £310

One of a set of six Victorian balloon backed handchairs, with carved and scrolled front legs and horsehair upholstered seats. $620 £310

One of a matched set of seven Yorkshire oak dining chairs. $640 £320

One of a set of eight 19th century mahogany dining chairs.
$650 £325

One of a set of five Sheraton mahogany dining chairs with reeded frames and spar backs, on square tapering legs. $660 £330

One of a set of six Chippendale style oak chairs, circa 1870. $660 £330

One of a set of six spindle bobbin doll's chairs, circa 1800. $660 £330

43

DINING CHAIRS

One of a set of six mahogany Regency style dining chairs, on sabre front legs.
$670 £335

One of a pair of old oak upright chairs with scrolled arched cresting rails.
$670 £335

One of a set of eleven spindle back chairs, country made. $680 £340

One of a set of six late 18th century Hepplewhite mahogany dining chairs. $700 £350

One of a set of four plus two small Queen Anne style walnut dining chairs.
$720 £360

One of a set of six Victorian walnut balloon back chairs. $720 £360

One of a set of six Victorian rosewood boudoir chairs. $740 £370

One of a set of four Victorian salon chairs in mahogany with centre oval padded back panels. $740 £370

One of a set of six, oak, country made, Hepplewhite dining chairs, circa 1800.
$780 £390

One of a set of eight mahogany dining chairs with drop in seat, circa 1825. $780 £390

One of a set of six decorative Victorian rosewood chairs on turned legs. $780 £390

One of a set of six simulated rosewood chairs, circa 1845. $800 £400

One of a set of eight George III mahogany dining chairs with carved and fluted spar backs. $800 £400

A fine early correction chair. $840 £420

One of a set of six early 18th century elm ladderback chairs. $860 £430

One of a set of six William and Mary style chairs, 19th century. $880 £440

One of a set of four Regency period mahogany chairs, circa 1810. $900 £450

One of a set of seven mid 19th century beechwood chairs, consisting of five diners and two easy chairs. $900 £450

DINING CHAIRS

One of a set of six 19th century mahogany dining chairs in Hepplewhite design. $940 £470

One of a set of four Sheraton period sabre leg chairs in faded mahogany, circa 1780. $950 £475

One of a set of six Regency mahogany chairs with bergere seats, the front inlaid with two bands of rosewood, circa 1830. $960 £480

One of a set of eight mahogany bar back chairs on turned legs, circa 1835. $960 £480

One of a set of six Chippendale carved mahogany dining chairs on cabriole legs with ball and claw feet. $960 £480

One of a set of six George III mahogany dining chairs. $1,010 £505

One of a set of eight oak chairs, mid 19th century, leather seat. $1,010 £505

One of a set of eight mahogany dining chairs with pierced splats and drop in seats, on cabriole legs with claw and ball feet (2 & 6). $1,060 £530

One of a pair of early George III mahogany chairs in the Chinese taste. $1,080 £540

One of a set of eight Georgian mahogany chairs in the Chippendale style, circa 1780. $1,080 £540

One of a set of six Regency sabre leg dining chairs in mahogany with ebony string inlay. $1,080 £540

One of a set of six rosewood dining chairs with Trafalgar seats, circa 1840. $1,100 £550

One of a set of eight late 18th century Chippendale style chairs. $1,100 £550

One of a set of four Adam style mahogany dining chairs. $1,100 £550

One of a set of six spindle back rush seated chairs, circa 1770. $1,140 £570

One of a set of seven Regency beechwood chairs, with an 'X' shaped splat on octagonal sabre legs. $1,140 £570

One of a set of ten Regency mahogany dining chairs. $1,150 £575

One of a set of six Regency mahogany dining chairs. $1,180 £590

47

DINING CHAIRS

One of a set of eight (6 singles, 2 carvers) early 19th century mahogany dining chairs. $1,180 £590

One of a set of six Continental high back chairs with cane seats and backs, 46in. high, circa 1790. $1,190 £595

An ebonised chair by Charles Rennie Mackintosh. $1,190 £595

One of a part set of five provincial Queen Anne walnut chairs. $1,200 £600

One of a set of six George III mahogany dining chairs. $1,200 £600

One of a pair of walnut chairs with inlaid stringing to the splat, circa 1690. $1,200 £600

One of a set of four George I oak chairs. $1,200 £600

17th century Dutch leather Delft chair on baluster legs, 19½in. wide. $1,250 £625

One of a set of six Regency mahogany dining chairs, the centre back rail with satinwood fern and central flower design. $1,380 £690

48

DINING CHAIRS

One of a set of four chairs by W. Morgan, heavily carved by S. Hobbis, circa 1850. $1,380 £690

One of a set of eight mahogany side chairs, the front cabriole legs with original brass swivel castors.$1,380 £690

One of a set of six carved oak, Charles II style chairs, 19th century with dished seats. $1,400 £700

One of a set of ten William IV rosewood dining chairs. $1,440 £720

One of a set of ten plus two Adam style mahogany dining chairs.$1,440 £720

One of a set of eight Hepplewhite style dining chairs.$1,440 £720

One of a set of six Regency sabre leg chairs with carved rope rails. $1,490 £745

One of a set of six early 19th century dining chairs on sabre legs with delicate marquetry inlay. $1,500 £750

One of a set of eight mahogany frame dining chairs with carved acanthus leaves at top of cabriole legs, circa 1840. $1,560 £780

49

DINING CHAIRS

One of a set of ten Regency rosewood dining chairs. $1,580 £790

One of a set of ten ladder back chairs in oak with re-rushed loose seats, circa 1850. $1,640 £820

One of a pair of late 18th century chairs, brass inlaid, with their toprail inset with a painted paper cameo portrait. $1,680 £840

One of a set of six George II red walnut dining chairs. $1,870 £935

One of a set of six Hepplewhite chairs. $1,920 £960

One of a set of eight late 17th century style dining chairs including two arm chairs. $1,920 £960

One of a pair of chairs by Charles Rennie Mackintosh. $1,920 £960

One of a set of eight mahogany dining chairs of George III design with carved and fluted spars to back, standing on square tapering legs. $1,980 £990

One of a set of six, late 18th century German or Dutch mahogany chairs. $1,980 £990

50

One of a set of six Georgian dining chairs. $2,040 £1,020

One of a set of six George II fruitwood chairs with leather seats, circa 1740. $2,110 £1,055

One of a set of twelve William IV dining chairs on turned and fluted legs. $2,160 £1,080

One of a pair of 17th century Italian gilt-wood chairs. $2,160 £1,080

One of a set of six Italian walnut chairs. $2,220 £1,110

One of a set of six mahogany dining chairs. $2,280 £1,140

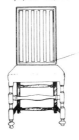

One of a set of twelve mahogany dining chairs, with pierced splats and fluted top rails and uprights. $2,400 £1,200

One of a set of eight William III walnut dining chairs. $2,640 £1,320

One of a set of eight Sheraton style dining chairs. $2,820 £1,410

DINING CHAIRS

One of a set of five George II walnut dining chairs. $2,860 £1,430

One of a set of twelve mahogany dining chairs of late 18th century design. $2,900 £1,450

One of a set of eight early 19th century satinwood chairs with gilt mounts. $3,080 £1,540

A small straight-back chair in ebonised wood, designed by Charles Rennie Mackintosh, 40in. high. $3,080 £1,540

One of a set of six walnut side chairs with cabriole front legs, circa 1710. $3,280 £1,640

One of a set of eight 17th century oak dining chairs. $3,300 £1,650

One of a set of six Dutch marquetry walnut single chairs. $3,520 £1,760

One of a set of six 'dropped toprail' mahogany dining chairs. $3,520 £1,760

One of a set of six Queen Anne fruitwood dining chairs with rush seats on cabriole legs with turned stretcher rails. $3,740 £1,870

One of a set of six late
18th century Italian
walnut chairs, heightened
in gilt. $4,620 £2,310

One of a set of eight
Henry II walnut
dining chairs. $4,620
£2,310

One of a set of twelve
Regency period car-
ved rosewood dining
chairs with sabre legs.
$4,620 £2,310

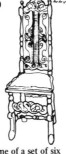

One of a set of six
walnut chairs with
fiddle back splats,
circa 1740. $5,500 £2,750

One of a set of six
James II dining chairs
with cane seats and
splats, circa 1685.$6,490 £3,245

One of a set of
twelve George IV
dining chairs.
$7,700 £3,850

One of a set of eight
Regency mahogany
dining chairs with
brass inlay.$8,250 £4,125

One of a set of fifteen
George III mahogany
dining chairs.
$16,500 £8,250

Harlequin set of
nine carved wal-
nut chairs.
$17,600 £8,800

DINING CHAIRS

Two of a set of four 19th century walnut and leather chairs, the back and seat edged with heavy brass studs, the legs and stretchers spiral turned. $220 £110

Two of a set of two arm and two single 19th century elm ladder back chairs. $140 £70

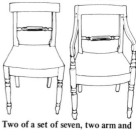

Two of a set of five Hepplewhite style chairs, three dining and two elbow. $260 £130

Two of a set of seven, two arm and five single, Victorian mahogany dining chairs. $290 £145

Two of a set of six 19th century mahogany dining chairs with spar backs and square tapered legs. $380 £190

Two of a set of six Edwardian inlaid mahogany dining chairs with shaped splats and cabriole legs. $430 £215

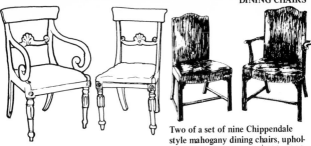

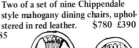

Two of a set of nine Chippendale style mahogany dining chairs, uphol-stered in red leather. $780 £390

Two of a set of eight 19th century bar back chairs on turned legs. $770 £385

Two of a set of ten (8 & 2) Orms-kirk ladder back chairs, circa 1820. $820 £410

Two of a set of eight mahogany in-laid dining chairs, two arm and six single. $910 £455

Two of a set of six mahogany chairs with 'Prince of Wales' carved backs, circa 1860. $1,070 £535

Two of a set of eight Chippendale style mahogany dining chairs with shaped top rails. $1,150 £575

DINING CHAIRS

Two of a set of six (4 & 2) early 18th century oak and yew wood chairs. $1,200 £600

Two of a set of eight Chippendale style mahogany dining chairs. $1,200 £600

Two of a set of ten reeded mahogany chairs, circa 1850. $1,220 £610

Two of a set of nine, eight single and one carver, Regency mahogany sabre leg chairs. $1,250 £625

Two of a set of six mahogany dining chairs with serpentine fronted seats. $1,320 £660

Two of a set of twelve, two arm and ten single, mahogany dining chairs with carved and pierced Gothic splats. $1,440 £720

Two of a set of eight (6 & 2) oak
Yorkshire wavy-line ladder back
chairs with rush seats, circa 1780.
$1,440 £720

Two of a set of eight early 19th century mahogany dining chairs.
$1,490 £745

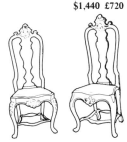

Pair of 18th century Portugese rosewood dining chairs. $1,680 £840

Two of a set of fourteen Victorian
oak chairs in the 'Jacobean' style.
$1,680 £840

Two of a set of eight (6 & 2) late
18th century mahogany chairs in
the Chippendale style. $1,800 £900

Two of a set of eight mahogany
dining chairs in Chippendale style,
circa 1870. $1,840 £920

DINING CHAIRS

Part of a set of six and two Hepple-white dining chairs in mahogany.
$2,400 £1,200

Two of a set of eight (6 & 2) Charles II style oak dining chairs, circa 1690.
$2,640 £1,320

Part of a set of eight 19th century dining chairs on cabriole legs.
$2,800 £1,400

Two of a set of eight (6 & 2) Cromwellian oak framed dining chairs. $3,080 £1,540

Two of a set of ten (8 & 2) Hepple-white mahogany stick-back chairs, circa 1780. $3,190 £1,595

Two of a set of twelve Chippendale period dining chairs with claw and ball feet. $3,960 £1,980

Two of a set of eight late 18th century Dutch marquetry dining chairs. $4,070 £2,035

Two of a set of six Cromwellian chairs. $4,620 £2,310

Two of a set of ten Hepplewhite carved mahogany dining chairs.
          $5,070 £2,535

Two of a fine set of eight Regency mahogany dining chairs, the backs lightly carved with leaf and reeded motifs, with rosewood panels inlaid with brass foliate scrolls and circular motifs. $5,720 £2,860

Two of a set of six Hepplewhite period mahogany chairs consisting of two carvers and four singles.
          $6,600 £3,300

Two of a set of twelve Chippendale design mahogany dining chairs.
          $8,360 £4,180

ARMLESS EASY CHAIRS

19th century lady's oak chair, on turned legs. $40 £20

Beech framed caned campaign chair. $40 £20

A lady's Victorian rosewood easy chair, the high panel back and seat in tapestry. $50 £25

A 19th century, lady's ebonised chair with upholstered panel back and seat. $100 £50

Victorian mahogany and iron framed chair on turned legs. $100 £50

A lady's Victorian walnut easy chair with upholstered panel back and seat, on turned legs. $110 £5

Wicker beach chair with hood. $116 £58

One of a pair of Hepplewhite easy chairs on tapered mahogany legs and stretchers. $130 £65

A Victorian mahogany chair, with rectangular back and seat, covered in floral needlework, on cabriole legs. $130 £65

Small Victorian
ebonised child's
chair. $144 £72

A lady's spoon back
easy chair, on rose-
wood scroll legs.
$160 £80

A Victorian lady's
chair covered in
sewed work, on
cabriole legs. $170 £85

Victorian lady's
carved mahogany
easy chair. $220 £110

Good quality early
Victorian walnut
lady's chair. $320 £160

A lady's Victorian car-
ved rosewood easy
chair, on cabriole legs,
upholstered in floral
beadwork. $350 £175

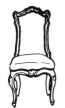

Louis XV style gilt-
wood easy chair
with carved cabriole
legs. $350 £175

Fine quality William and
Mary chair upholstered
in gold velvet, circa 1690.
$960 £480

A late 18th century
Indo-Portugese
padouk wood burgo-
master chair.
$1,080 £540

61

OPEN ARM EASY CHAIRS

Late 19th century folding chair with carpet back and seat. $40 £20

Victorian mahogany open sided arm chair. $60 £30

Late Victorian wicker chair. $60 £30

A mahogany bergere chair, with cane back and sides, on claw and ball feet. $68 £34

Late 19th century carved mahogany arm chair. $72 £36

One of a pair of late 19th century mahogany framed arm chairs on turned legs. $84 £42

A Victorian mahogany arm easy chair, the back and seat covered in crimson rep. $110 £55

A Victorian stained and carved arm chair on spiral legs and stretchers. $110 £55

A Victorian carved oak arm chair, the high panel back, arms and seat covered in velvet. $116 £58

An oak arm chair in the William and Mary manner. $120 £60

Edwardian inlaid mahogany circle back arm chair on square tapered legs. $120 £60

An Edwardian mahogany business arm chair, the panel back and seat covered in brown leather, on cabriole legs. $120 £60

Victorian carved walnut high back arm chair. $120 £60

19th century Italian style black painted open arm chair with scroll legs and stretchers. $144 £72

Victorian mahogany open sided arm chair on turned and fluted front legs. $144 £72

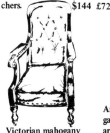

A mahogany arm chair in George III style, with an oval padded back and padded arms, with moulded scroll supports. $160 £80

Victorian mahogany open sided buttoned back arm chair. $160 £80

An Edwardian mahogany inlaid circle back arm chair with sparred back and sides, on square tapered legs. $170 £85

63

OPEN ARM EASY CHAIRS

A 19th century mahogany arm chair of Louis XV design, on fluted cabriole legs. $180 £90

One of a pair of Victorian rosewood chairs with spiral arms, legs and stretchers. $190 £95

A Victorian papier mache and mother-of-pearl inlaid spoon back arm chair, on cabriole legs. $220 £1[...]

Early Victorian rosewood button back grandfather chair, with original brass castors. $230 £115

A Regency scroll back mahogany frame chair, upholstered in red and green brocade. $230 £115

A fine Victorian open sided arm chair in rosewood with cabriole legs and scroll feet. $240 £120

Child's chair made from fourteen cow horns with velvet upholstered seat, 18in. high, 13in. wide, circa 1835. $240 £120

Victorian turned leg, grandfather chair in walnut. $240 £120

William IV mahogany arm chair covered in tan leather. $290 £145

A French giltwood salon chair, carved in the Louis XVI manner. $290 £145

Victorian button back, walnut framed easy chair. $300 £150

French empire style bergere chair. $340 £170

George III mahogany framed arm chair on finely turned legs with an 'H' stretcher. $340 £170

A 19th century mahogany framed invalid's chair, with adjustable back and pull out foot rest. $350 £175

Finely carved rosewood Victorian grandfather chair with cabriole legs. $350 £175

Early 19th century carved walnut arm chair, 39in. high. $370 £185

French Provincial walnut framed arm chair. $390 £195

Large Edwardian library chair, in green hide. $420 £210

OPEN ARM EASY CHAIRS

Georgian mahogany
library chair on
shaped legs. $500 £250

Superb quality
Chippendale style
library chair,
circa 1840. $600 £300

One of a pair of
Italian walnut
arm chairs. $620 £310

17th century carved
oak wainscot chair.
$640 £320

18th century uphol-
stered easy chair on
cabriole legs. $670 £335

One of a pair of
Louis XV easy
chairs. $720 £360

One of a pair of
Louis XVI style
giltwood fauteuils.
$720 £360

One of a pair of
Edwardian wicker
garden chairs.
$770 £385

Hepplewhite elbow
chair with cabriole
legs. $770 £385

A George II mahogany framed library chair. $840 £420

Louis XV gilt fauteuil, signed Falconet. $860 £430

Late 17th century walnut framed chair upholstered with gros point covers, on turned front supports with bun feet. $900 £450

One of a pair of French style walnut open arm chairs on cabriole legs. $910 £455

18th century Continental walnut scroll arm easy chair on cabriole legs. $1,010 £505

Late 18th century Adam design carved open arm chair on turned legs. $1,020 £510

A mid Georgian carved mahogany Gainsborough chair, the curved arm supports terminating in carved acanthus leaf finials. $1,060 £530

One of a set of six William and Mary walnut chairs. $1,060 £530

One of a pair of Regency gilt and rosewood chairs. $1,060 £530

67

OPEN ARM EASY CHAIRS

A rare Regency fruitwood fauteuil. $1,260 £630

One of a pair of 19th century Chippendale style chairs. $1,320 £660

One of a pair of mid 19th century oak thrones with tall arched backs and the arms on arcaded supports. $1,440 £720

A Flemish walnut master's chair, supported on cabriole legs, circa 1700, 58in. high. $1,440 £720

Late 19th century Chinese chair, part of a set including another chair and a settle, 49in. wide. $1,510 £755

A rare collapsible military campaign chair, circa 1770. $1,560 £78

One of a pair of painted, Sheraton elbow chairs. $1,680 £840

Mid 18th century mahogany framed open arm chair. $1,680 £840

One of a pair of Adam style giltwood arm chairs, one original circa 1772, the other an identical copy circa 1972, 37in. high. $1,800 £900

One of a set of six
Victorian walnut
arm chairs, on
cabriole legs. $1,800 £900

Late 17th century
Venetian Baroque
giltwood arm chair.
$2,160 £1,080

One of a suite of
four fauteuils of
Louis XV design.
$2,400 £1,200

One of a pair of maho-
gany framed mid
Georgian arm chairs on
cabriole legs. $3,740 £1,870

One of a suite of four
Louis XV fauteuils by
Nogaret of Lyon.
$6,120 £3,060

One of a pair of
18th century
carved giltwood
chairs in Louis
XV style. $11,000
£5,500

Early 18th century,
Louis XIV carved
walnut fauteuil.
$14,300 £7,150

One of a pair of English,
Queen Anne arm chairs in
walnut with needlework
seat and back.
$15,000 £7,500

One of a set of four
George II mahogany
arm chairs, with cab-
riole legs and ball
and claw feet.
$19,800 £9,900

69

UPHOLSTERED ARM EASY CHAIRS

A high back upholstered arm easy chair on turned legs with club feet.
$60 £30

A Victorian easy chair in blue and white crettone, with a slip cover.
$72 £36

Late 19th century upholstered arm chair on short turned legs. $72 £36

An Edwardian ebonised arm chair, on short cabriole legs. $84 £42

Late 19th century walnut framed upholstered arm chair on brass castors.
$84 £42

A lady's small easy chair, upholstered in green floral figured brocade, on turned legs. $100 £50

A rosewood circle back easy chair, on carved turned legs. $110 £55

Early 20th century high backed arm chair, upholstered in green and silver weave. $110 £55

Edwardian inlaid mahogany easy chair on short tapered legs with spade feet. $110 £55

70

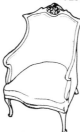

Victorian upholstered arm chair on turned legs. $120 £60

Mahogany framed circle back easy chair. $120 £60

Victorian buttoned back chair on short turned legs with brass and glass ball castors. $130 £65

One of a pair of small upholstered easy chairs. $144 £72

Edwardian inlaid mahogany easy chair on short cabriole legs. $144 £72

Shell shaped Victorian button back bedroom chair. $160 £80

A Victorian, oak, spoon back easy chair, standing on cabriole legs.
$170 £85

Victorian iron framed buttoned back,lady's chair on turned legs with brass castors.
$190 £95

An Oriental carved and pierced circle back easy chair on scroll legs, the upholstered seat in rep.
$200 £100

UPHOSTERED ARM EASY CHAIRS

A Victorian mahogany spoon back easy chair, with button back, standing on cabriole legs. $260 £130

Gentleman's Victorian mahogany easy chair on turned legs. $280 £140

Victorian carved walnut and upholstered, father's chair with shaped, scrolled balloon type back, on cabriole legs. $300 £15

Victorian papier mache occasional chair, with mother-of-pearl and painted decoration.
$300 £150

A fine Victorian shaped back, gent's chair, on cabriole legs. $350 £175

Early 19th century French style giltwood chair. $370 £18

Louis XVI style bergere chair with carved giltwood frame. $370 £185

Gentleman's Victorian mahogany easy chair.
$370 £185

Louis XVI bergere chair on fluted legs. $410 £205

Early 19th century buttoned arm chair, upholstered in leather with fluted legs and brass castors. $480 £240

Victorian carved mahogany easy chair on cabriole legs. $530 £265

18th century hide arm chair on cabriole legs with scroll and leaf motifs and ball and claw feet. $720 £360

One of a pair of interesting heavily carved Oriental hardwood arm chairs. $790 £395

Early 19th century rosewood arm chair, upholstered in leather. $1,150 £575

Gainsborough library chair upholstered in hide, circa 1760. $1,800 £900

English, 18th century carved and gilt wood chair. $1,800 £900

One of a rare pair of Louis XV large fauteuils stamped J. Blanchard. $21,000 £10,500

American library arm chair attributed to Duncan Phyfe, circa 1815. $26,600 £13,300

HALL CHAIRS

Victorian Gothic style carved oak hall chair. $40 £20

Victorian mahogany hall chair on turned front legs. $50 £25

A Victorian carved mahogany hall arm chair. $100 £50

19th century Continental oak hall chairs. $100 £50

A highly carved Victorian oak hall chair. $120 £60

Continental walnut hall chair profusely carved with cherubs and scrolls. $190 £95

One of a pair of good 19th century mahogany hall chairs with painted stag's head crests. $240 £120

A 19th century mahogany hall chair. $360 £180

One of a pair of 17th century Italian hall chairs, 3ft.7in. high. $960 £480

An unusual Edwardian, child's high chair. $72 £36

19th century Windsor wheel back child's high chair in figured elm. $110 £55

Early 19th century elm, lacemaker's chair. $144 £72

Early Victorian child's high chair and stand of dark mahogany $170 £85

Child's elm high chair complete with adjustable step, circa 1820. $180 £90

Regency period mahogany, child's chair and stand. $290 £145

Chippendale period fruitwood child's chair of good colour and condition, 37in. high. $350 £175

Child's oak high chair, circa 1680, with one new stretcher. $580 £290

Charles II walnut high chair with twist supports. $1,800 £900

NURSING CHAIRS

Regency period black and gilt nursing chair. $72 £36

Victorian upholstered nursing chair on turned legs with brass castors. $72 £36

A lady's small satin-walnut circle back nursing chair, with panel back and seat in velour. $84 £42

Small Victorian nursing chair on short turned legs. $120 £60

Victorian lady's nursing chair in walnut with a pierced splat back and turned legs. $144 £72

Small Victorian upholstered nursing chair on short turned legs. $160 £80

19th century inlaid walnut nursing chair. $180 £90

Small Victorian walnut nursing chair on turned legs. $220 £110

Victorian walnut framed nursing chair upholstered in the original bead and needlework cover. $260 £13

Victorian rosewood
framed prie dieu chair
on short turned legs.
$84 £42

Victorian mahogany
framed prie dieu chair
with turned front
supports. $110 £55

Victorian walnut
framed prie dieu
chair with cabriole
leg supports. $120 £60

An unusual Victorian
French style prie dieu
chair on fluted legs.
$130 £65

Victorian rosewood prie
dieu chair, with original
buttoned coffee brown
upholstery, circa 1845.
$160 £80

Victorian walnut
devotional chair
on cabriole legs.
$190 £95

19th century
cabriole legged
prie dieu chair
in walnut. $240 £120

Victorian papier
mache prie dieu
chair. $240 £120

Early 18th century
Italian prie dieu in-
laid with ivory.
$1,920 £960

ROCKING CHAIRS

A child's Shetland rocking arm chair. $60 £30

A late 19th century mahogany framed rocking chair, upholstered in fawn moquette. $80 £40

Victorian beechwood rocking chair. $90 £45

A Victorian rocking chair with spindle spar back. $100 £50

Late 19th century child's bentwood rocking chair. $110 £55

A teak rocking arm chair with cane back and seat. $120 £60

19th century elm ladderback rocker with a rush seat. $160 £80

Elm rocking chair with rush seat, circa 1800. $160 £80

Late 19th century mahogany rocking chair. $160 £80

Lancashire fruitwood
rocking chair with ash-
wood turnings, circa
1820. $164 £82

Victorian bentwood
rocking chair with a
cane seat and back.
              $190 £95

A countrymade rock-
ing chair with bobbin
turned splats, circa
1830. $190 £95

Early 19th century
elm rocking chair
of a good honey
colour. $190 £95

Early 19th century
farmhouse rocker
in fruitwood with
a pistol drawer.
              $220 £110

American rocking chair
with the original painted
decoration, 42in. high,
circa 1840. $240 £120

Small 18th century
mahogany rocking
chair, 2ft.6in. high.
$240 £120

Victorian steel-
framed rocking
chair with leather
upholstery. $310 £155

Late 19th century
child's rocker in
mahogany. $720 £360

SETTEES AND COUCHES

A Victorian mahogany half back couch, on turned, fluted legs.
$150 £75

Satinwood inlaid arm settee with pierced splat and panel back.
$170 £85

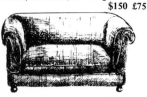

Victorian two-seater chesterfield (needs recovering). $190 £95

A mahogany framed arm settee on square tapered legs, upholstered in floral tapestry. $190 £95

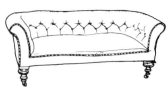

Victorian settee with circle back on turned legs. $190 £95

Cast iron garden seat with pierced scroll back, arms, seat and legs, 5ft. wide. $200 £100

Edwardian pale mahogany open sided settee on cabriole leg supports. $200 £100

Edwardian inlaid mahogany settee on tapering legs with spade feet.
$200 £100

Victorian scroll back chaise longue on turned legs. $200 £100

A cast iron garden seat with pierced fern leaf back and arms and sparred wood seat, 5ft. wide. $220 £110

Victorian arm settee buttoned in green velvet, 2.23m. wide. $220 £110

An Edwardian mahogany framed settee, upholstered in a Regency stripe material. $240 £120

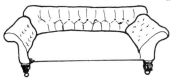

19th century mahogany framed hall seat in the Gothic style, 5ft. 2in. wide. $240 £120

Edwardian inlaid mahogany couch on cabriole legs. $240 £120

A Georgian walnut framed three-seater settee, 5ft. 3in. wide. $260 £130

A 19th century carved rosewood settee with two scroll arms, upholstered in damask, on turned legs. $290 £145

81

SETTEES AND COUCHES

A white painted settee in Regency style, with padded back and scrolling arms faced with brass paternae and acanthus carving, 7ft.6in. long. $300 £150

Small 19th century giltwood settee on turned and fluted legs, 4ft.3in. wide. $290 £145

Victorian turned leg chaise longue in mahogany. $300 £150

Late 19th century giltwood settee of small proportions. $310 £155

Victorian mahogany settee on cabriole legs, 4ft.6in. wide. $310 £155

A Continental carved and ebonised arm settee with carved splats and mounts of lion masks and child's head, on turned baluster legs, 4ft. 10in. wide. $320 £160

19th century Continental fruitwood couch, 6ft.2in. long. $340 £170

18th century Continental fruitwood bench. $340 £170

19th century two-seater settee with cane sides, back and seat in the French style. $340 £170

French carved walnut arm settee on cabriole legs, 175cm. wide. $350
£175

A small Louis XV design carved giltwood arm settee on cabriole legs. $350 £175

A Regency mahogany settee with scroll arms, a panel back, squab cushion and scroll legs, 6ft.6in. wide. $360 £180

A square back arm settee on mahogany square tapered legs, 189cm. $360 £180

19th century mahogany circle back wing settee on cabriole legs, the frame carved with flowers and scrolls. $360 £180

19th century rosewood framed scroll end sofa on turned legs, 5ft.3in. long. $360 £180

Victorian rosewood barley twist framed couch with button backrest and turned feet with brass castors. $360 £180

SETTEES AND COUCHES

19th century upholstered and gilt-wood sofa in the Louis XV style.
$400 £200

A 19th century mahogany settee in George II style, the back and seat covered in floral needlework, the arms terminating in scrolls, 6ft.4in. long. $420 £210

Louis XV style gilt and white settee on cabriole legs. $420 £210

19th century Oriental hardwood settee, profusely carved. $430 £215

A Victorian mahogany sofa with shaped half panel back, on fluted cabriole legs, 6ft. long. $430 £215

Victorian shaped front settee on fine ebonised legs with brass castors. $430 £215

Fine Victorian couch with cabriole legs. $430 £215

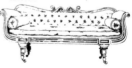

William IV scroll end sofa in mahogany with ebony banding.
$480 £240

Mid 18th century French giltwood settee, 5ft. 8in. long. $480 £240

Victorian carved mahogany framed, shaped back settee, 7ft. wide.
$480 £240

Victorian carved walnut frame chaise longue on cabriole legs. $500 £250

A carved mahogany framed bergere suite with cane sides and backs, and upholstered seats and cushions, standing on cabriole legs, comprising a settee and two easy chairs. $520 £260

An elaborately carved Continental locker seat. $480 £240

Victorian rosewood framed couch on cabriole legs, with a shaped and buttoned back. $480 £240

Regency rosewood and brass inlaid settee, 8ft. 3in. wide. $500 £250

Louis XVI style giltwood couch on fluted legs. $510 £255

SETTEES AND COUCHES

19th century, highly carved, Burmese teak double ended chaise longue, decorated with animals and scrolls. $520 £260

Late 19th century reproduction mahogany settee carved with Prince of Wales feathers, 4ft. 9in. long. $540 £270

Regency period scroll end sofa in rosewood with sabre legs. $540 £270

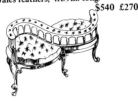

19th century love seat on delicately carved cabriole legs. $540 £270

18th century oak triple chair back settee, 62in. wide. $550 £275

An attractive simulated rosewood couch of the Regency period with ormolu mounts. $600 £300

Ebonised Empire style chaise longue with painted decoration. $600 £300

A good quality scroll end sofa of the Regency period in rosewood, with sabre legs and brass claw castors. $620 £310

Good quality Victorian walnut framed settee on turned legs with a finely carved centre back. $620 £310

Victorian, walnut framed, double-backed settee, standing on turned legs. $620 £310

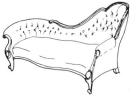

Victorian carved walnut spoon back settee on cabriole legs. $620 £310

Mid 18th century Continental gilt-wood triple back settee with cane back and seat. $640 £320

A Victorian walnut framed, double-end settee. $640 £320

Victorian walnut framed settee with open arms and cabriole legs, 5ft.6in. wide. $710 £355

Burmese settee of serpentine shape extensively carved and pierced. $720 £360

Early 19th century brass inlaid mahogany framed settee on sabre legs with brass castors. $720 £360

SETTEES AND COUCHES

A Moresque hardwood double seat, with tortoiseshell and mother-of-pearl inlay. $720 £360

A small good quality Regency period rosewood settee on sabre legs with brass claw feet and brass inlay. $770 £385

Victorian walnut framed sociable settee. $770 £385

19th century reproduction triple chair back settee. $780 £390

Walnut frame settee of George II design with rectangular back and paw feet , 46 ins. high . $790 £395

Victorian mahogany framed button back settee supported on cabriole legs. $820 £410

A French carved walnut chaise longue of Louis XV design, in three parts. $840 £420

Satinwood sofa with painted decorations, 59 x 21 x 33in. high, circa 1800. $840 £420

English wrought iron seat in
Chippendale style, about 1760.
$900 £450

Victorian walnut framed ottoman
with serpentine shaped seats, on
cabriole legs. $910 £455

Chippendale period mahogany
framed settee, 5ft.2in. long. $960 £480

A fine quality Victorian walnut
framed sofa with decorative
ormolu mounts. $960 £480

Gothic style sofa and steps, 2ft.6in.
high, circa 1820. $960 £480

17th century Spanish chestnut wood
seat, 73in. wide. $1,020 £510

Late 19th century three seater
Chesterfield covered in brown hide.
$1,060 £530

Caned mahogany couch, circa 1810,
72in. wide. $1,180 £590

89

SETTEES AND COUCHES

Early 19th century double chair back settee, in walnut. $1,200 £600

19th century French giltwood settee on cabriole legs with scroll feet. $1,320 £660

A good quality 19th century Louis XV style giltwood chaise longue in the form of a pair of chairs with shaped stool to match. $1,340 £670

French style carved and painted conversation settee, circa 1850.
$1,380 £690

Part of a late 19th century five-piece Burmese hardwood suite comprising settee, two open arm chairs, and two single chairs, all heavily carved and pierced with dragon designs. $1,440 £720

Part of a three-piece suite of Art Deco silvered furniture. $1,560 £780

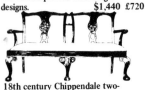

18th century Chippendale two-chair back settee of excellent colour and condition. $1,680 £840

Queen Anne walnut settee, 6ft. wide.
$1,800 £900

Good quality late 18th century mahogany sofa with satinwood inlay and fine turned legs. $1,800 £900

Upholstered swing seat, 90in. tall, circa 1880, made in India. $2,160 £1,080

English gilt wood and plaster settee of shaped oval form, divided into four sections, about 1830. $2,160 £1,080

18th century Gothic style mahogany couch on claw feet. $2,420 £1,210

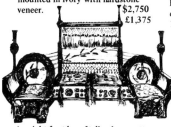

A rare Bishop's triple-seated throne, mounted in ivory with hardstone veneer. $2,750 £1,375

Rosewood, satinwood and teak carved settee with cane seat, about 1700, 59½in. long. $4,840 £2,420

An eight foot long Italian banquette, part of a suite by Carlo Bugatti. $13,000 £6,500

A superb gondola sofa by Marcel Goard. $28,000 £14,000

91

SETTLES

A carved oak hall settle, with carved lion mask arm terminals and box seat, 4ft. wide. $240 £120

19th century carved oak settle with a cane back and lift up seat. $300 £15

19th century pine table settle, the top of which folds back to make a seat, 59in. wide. $360 £180

Oak settle with fielded panels, 22 x 71 x 43in. high, circa 1710. $380 £19

Late 18th century carved oak monk's bench, with a lift-up seat. $400 £200

Late 18th century Welsh oak settle with a box seat. $410 £205

Excellent curved pine settle, circa 1840, 4ft. wide. $470 £235

Early 19th century Welsh bacon settle in elm. $480 £240

A carved oak hall settle, 56in. long. $620 £310

French Provincial oak hall settle with box seat and scroll arms. $620 £310

17th century oak table settle of good colour. $1,440 £720

Late 17th century highly decorated Northern English oak settle with a plank rear. $1,460 £730

93

STEP CHAIRS

19th century oak library chair steps. $50 £25

Victorian mahogany chair steps. $60 £30

Set of Gothic style oak library steps, 1850, 13in. wide. $144 £72

19th century oak library steps with tooled leather seat and treads. $350 £175

Early Victorian mahogany scroll arm chair which converts into library steps. $500 £250

Regency mahogany library steps with brass fittings. $640 £320

Regency library chair steps in mahogany, 35in. high, 21in. wide. circa 1820. $640 £320

Regency mahogany library chair steps, the steps with inset tooled leather, 35in. high. $1,020 £510

Regency giltwood steps, 25in. wide. $1,560 £780

Beechwood child's stool on turned legs. $24 £12

Edwardian ebonised stool on turned legs. $36 £18

19th century oak hall seat on turned legs. $36 £18

An Edwardian mahogany dressing stool, 1ft.10in. wide, on tapered legs. $54 £27

African carved teak circular stool with ten legs, 16½in. $54 £27

A mahogany stool, the square needle-work covered top raised on ring turned legs. $72 £36

Late 19th century carved walnut dressing table stool. $72 £36

19th century Ashanti Chieftain's stool, carved from a single piece of wood. $110 £55

Victorian cabriole leg dressing table stool, 1ft.10in. wide. $110 £55

STOOLS

A 19th century oblong dressing stool, on carved cabriole legs, with claw and ball feet. $110 £55

Elegant Regency period ebonised stool. $120 £60

A Victorian rosewood square stool, on spiral legs and stretchers, the seat covered in needlework. $120 £60

A 19th century dressing stool, on carved cabriole legs and paw feet. $160 £80

An early oak stool of Gothic design. $170 £85

Carved pine stool of the Regency period with original needlework seat. $170 £85

Camerons' Bekon Chief's circular stool the top supported by four natives and two animal figures. $230 £115

Late 18th century Hepplewhite stool. $300 £150

A Queen Anne oak close stool with simulated drawers. $300 £150

A large Victorian carved serpentine shaped stool, on cabriole legs, 4ft.6in. long. $310 £155

Late 18th century Chinese Chippendale style stool. $400 £200

A late 19th century Chinese mother-of-pearl inlaid padouk wood stool, with marble in-set top, 1ft.2in. diam. $400 £200

19th century Chinese porcelain garden seat, 17¾in. high. $820 £410

Queen Anne walnut stool, 1ft.10½in. x 1ft.4½in. $960 £480

African hardwood Chieftain's stool of Yoruba origin, single plank top adzed underneath, 23½ in. long, 15½in. high. $1,140 £570.

A superb Regency stool with carved gilt rope feet. $2,860 £1,430

Chippendale mahogany stool, circa 1760, 18½in. high. $2,900 £1,450

One of a pair of fine Queen Anne stools, 17½in. high. $7,700 £3,850 .

DUET STOOLS

French style walnut duet stool on cabriole legs, seat covered in printed cretonne. $100 £50

A Victorian walnut duet stool on cabriole legs, 3ft.5in. wide. $200 £10

19th century French style rosewood duet stool, circa 1840, 48in. long. $240 £120

A Victorian walnut oblong duet stool on cabriole legs, the box seat covered in blue rep, 4ft.1in. wide. $340 £170

FENDER STOOLS

A Victorian ottoman box stool, the seat covered in floral sewed work, 3ft.6in. wide. $100 £50

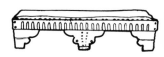

Early 17th century oak fire stool with leather top, 3ft.5in. long. $470 £235

Very rare Queen Anne veneered walnut hearth stool of fine honey colour, 41in. x 9½in. x 6in. $500 £250

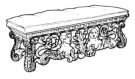

One of a pair of stools attributed to William Kent, of carved giltwood, 1.4m. wide. $11,000 £5,500

98

An Edwardian, rush-seated, oblong foot-stool. $14 £7

Mid 19th century stool in walnut with a fretted base. $24 £12

Mahogany scroll shaped footstool. $30 £15

Small Victorian uphol-stered footstool on bun feet. $30 £15

Victorian mahogany serpentine shaped footstool, on cabriole legs, 13in. wide. $34 £17

Victorian walnut framed footstool with a padded woolwork top, circa 1850. $48 £24

A stool made from an elephant's foot, with upholstered seat. $60 £30

Late 19th century mahogany foot-stool. $60 £30

Carved walnut French style oval footstool, covered in green vel-vet. $68 £34

Small Regency rosewood footstool. $96 £48

An unusual Victorian footstool made from elk's feet with an oak top. $110 £55

Chippendale design stool on carved cab-riole legs, 23½ x 16½in. $360 £180

JOINT STOOLS

19th century repro-
duction oak joint
stool. $110 £55

19th century oak
joint stool, 1ft.4in.
high. $120 £60

17th century style
oak joint stool.
$144 £72

Jacobean carved oak
oblong joint stool on
turned legs and stret-
chers, 45cm. wide.
$180 £90

A mid 17th century oak
stool, with moulded
seat raised on turned
columner legs, 1ft.3in.
$240 £120

17th century oak
joint stool, of
good colour.
$280 £140

18th century oak
joint stool. $290 £145

17th century oak
joint stool. $300 £150

Early oak joint
stool of good
colour. $310 £155

17th century oak
joint stool. $320 £160

English yew tree joint
stool, circa 1640, 23in.
high, with good turnings
and fine patination.
$480 £240

A good 17th century
oak joint stool,
standing on turned
legs. $480 £240

An Elizabethan oak
joint stool, maker's
mark I.A., 1ft.6½in.
wide. $670 £335

Charles I oak
joint stool,
1ft.5in. wide.
$840 £420

Late 16th century
French oak joint
stool, 2ft.2½in.
high. $1,080 £540

Late Elizabethan oak
joint stool, 1ft.7in.
wide. $1,320 £660

Late Elizabethan oak
joint stool, 1ft.6½in.
wide. $1,680 £840

One of a pair of
Charles I oak joint
stools, 1ft.5½in.
wide. $4,400 £2,200

PIANO STOOLS

Edwardian mahogany piano stool with an upholstered seat and cabriole legs. $44 £22

19th century cabriole leg mahogany piano stool with an upholstered lift-up top. $50 £25

Late 19th century circular mahogany revolving piano stool on square tapering legs. $50 £25

A mahogany inlaid oblong piano stool on square tapered legs. $60 £30

Early Victorian rosewood piano stool on a platform base with scroll feet. $60 £30

Victorian rosewood adjustable piano stool. $60 £30

Edwardian inlaid mahogany piano stool, 1ft.9in. wide. $60 £30

Victorian mahogany revolving piano stool. $60 £30

Edwardian piano stool on shaped legs with hoof feet. $72 £36

A rosewood inlaid music stool on cabriole legs, the hinged box seat covered in silk brocade. $80 £40

Bamboo piano stool, dated 1890. $88 £44

Victorian wind-up piano stool, upholstered in dralon. $96 £48

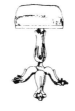

A 19th century piano stool, the linen covered seat resting on four tubular brass legs and central expanding pole. $120 £60

Good quality early Victorian rosewood piano stool with paw feet. $120 £60

An unusual Victorian mahogany music stool with adjustable seat. $200 £100

Unusual Regency period revolving piano stool. $200 £100

Victorian, adjustable, rosewood music seat with lyre-shaped splat. $300 £150

Rare Wedgewood spinette stool, 18in. high. $960 £480

WINDOW SEATS

Walnut and marquetry inlaid window seat with scroll arms, 2ft. 6in. wide. $130 £65

Sheraton style mahogany box strung and upholstered lyre-shaped window seat. $144 £72

Regency satinwood window seat with painted decoration. $310 £155

Hepplewhite period mahogany window seat. $380 £190

Hepplewhite period mahogany window seat. $420 £210

A window seat in the Chippendale manner with scrolled ends and gros point needlework, 4ft. long. $1,010 £505

A George II window seat. $1,680 £840

Early 19th century window seat in the manner of Duncan Phyfe. $2,640 £1,320

One of a pair of Louis XV cream painted and gilt decorated window seats. $2,640 £1,320

Edwardian inlaid
mahogany 'X'
shaped piano stool.
    $110 £55

Early 19th century
mahogany 'X' frame
stool. $120 £60

19th century simulated
rosewood 'X' frame
stool with woolwork
cover. $130 £65

Early 19th century
simulated rosewood
dressing stool. $190 £95

Regency 'X' frame
rosewood stool with
cane seat. $230 £115

Early 19th century
carved giltwood
stool on paw feet.
    $260 £130

Regency lacquered
and upholstered 'X'
frame stool, circa
1825. $310 £155

Regency giltwood
stool on paw feet.
    $360 £180

Mid 19th century
Victorian brass 'X'
framed stool, 1854,
29in. wide.
    $2,800 £1,400

105

SUITES

Late 19th century mahogany open sided three piece suite on fine turned legs terminating in brass castors. $260 £130

A carved mahogany drawing room suite, on cabriole legs, comprising an arm settee, two arm chairs and four single chairs. $310 £155

Edwardian mahogany inlaid drawing room suite of settee and two easy chairs. $410 £205

English cast iron seat with two chairs decorated in the fern pattern,
about 1870-80, seat 4ft.6in. wide, chair 2ft. wide. $480 £240

Edwardian inlaid rosewood drawing room suite of armed settee and two
easy chairs and four inlaid single chairs (seven pieces in all). $650 £325

A nine piece Edwardian mahogany drawing room suite comprising a
settee, two arm chairs, four dining chairs and two nursing chairs. $660 £330

SUITES

Part of a carved mahogany drawing room suite on cabriole legs, comprising an arm settee, two gentleman's arm chairs, two lady's chairs and four single chairs. $720 £360

An Edwardian mahogany, ivory inlaid, drawing room suite, comprising a low backed settee, a bergere and four side chairs, all with floral medallions and cabriole legs. $820 £410

Part of a late 19th century Victorian mahogany drawing room suite of seven pieces. $840 £420

108

Mahogany framed bergere suite with cane backs and sides and flowered silk damask cushions. $890 £445

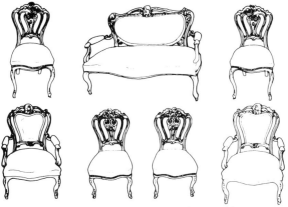

Victorian carved mahogany drawing room suite, comprising a settee, two arm chairs and four single chairs. $960 £480

Mid 19th century mahogany three-piece suite, comprising a couch, lady's chair and gent's chair. $1,200 £600

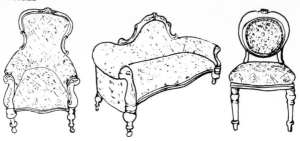

Victorian carved mahogany parlour suite comprising a settee, an easy chair and six single chairs. $1,250 £625

A fine 19th century mahogany framed three piece suite comprising a three seater settee and a pair of matching chairs with serpentine fronts and cabriole legs. $1,620 £810

Part of a suite of English satinwood seat furniture, comprising also a pair of arm chairs and four side chairs, circa 1900. $1,870 £935

19th century Louis XV style giltwood bergere suite comprising a two seater couch and two chairs. $2,040 £1,020

Early 19th century Empire style three piece suite. $2,200 £1,100

Late 19th century mahogany salon suite with painted decoration, on tapered legs with spade feet. $2,300 £1,150

A superb Victorian walnut suite comprising a double ended settee
with a medallion centre, a pair of arm chairs and a set of six cabriole
leg dining chairs. $2,400 £1,200

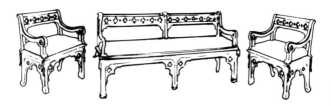

Part of a suite of Victorian Gothic revival seat furniture, about 1845.
                                                            $2,430 £1,215

A five piece French natural walnut suite, comprising a settee, two
single chairs and two arm chairs, upholstered in blue tapestry, circa
1860. $2,640 £1,320

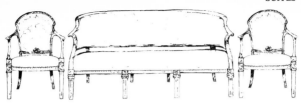

A good Louis XVI style suite comprising four arm chairs and a three
seat settee. $2,860 £1,430

An Adam style drawing room suite comprising circle back settee,
four dining chairs and two arm chairs, with the frames painted,
carved and fluted. $3,520 £1,760

A fine late 18th century giltwood three piece suite comprising a
settee and a pair of chairs. $3,530 £1,765

113

Part of a Dutch salon suite, settee and six singles. $3,630 £1,815

Part of a superb eleven piece Louis XVI salon suite. $8,800 £4,400

Part of a set of twelve George II seat furniture. $8,800 £4,400

Part of a French giltwood chateau suite of Louis XV design, comprising a canape, four fauteuils, banquette stool, firescreen and three-fold screen. $14,500 £7,250

An 18th century Franco-Flemish neo-classical giltwood suite de salon of a canape and eleven fauteuils. $20,000 £10,000

Three silver-mounted arm chairs, part of a set of Indian, late 19th century furniture, which also included the settee and stool.
$23,000 £11,500

TUB CHAIRS

Edwardian mahogany open sided arm chair on turned legs. $50 £25

A mahogany circle back arm chair on cabriole legs. $60 £30

A late 19th century circle back easy chair with upholstered back, arms and seat. $60 £30

Edwardian inlaid tub chair on turned legs. $60 £30

Edwardian ebonised frame tub shaped chair on short cabriole legs. $70 £35

Victorian rosewood circle back arm chair covered in green velvet on turned legs. $72 £36

Edwardian inlaid mahogany tub chair on cabriole legs. $84 £42

Edwardian mahogany framed arm chair with padded arms and short cabriole legs. $96 £48

Edwardian inlaid mahogany tub shaped elbow chair on square tapering legs. $96 £48

Victorian bobbin
framed tub chair.
$96 £48

Late Victorian horse-
shoe backed ebonised
occasional chair on
fluted legs. $110 £55

Late Victorian horse-
shoe back smoker's
chair in mahogany
with turned legs.
$110 £55

Edwardian inlaid
mahogany tub
shaped elbow
chair on tapered
legs. $116 £58

19th century maho-
gany sewing chair.
$144 £72

A Victorian mahogany
chair with buttoned
tub back, above ser-
pentine seat-rail, on
cabriole legs. $180 £90

18th century bamboo
tub shaped arm chair
with a caned seat.
$650 £325

One of a pair of carved
padouk wood swivel
tub chairs. $1,250 £625

Early 18th century
walnut arm chair of
superb colour.
$2,280 £1,140

117

WING CHAIRS

A small carved mahogany wing easy chair on cabriole legs. $72 £36

One of a pair of Victorian upholstered arm chairs on bun feet. $72 £36

Edwardian inlaid mahogany framed wing arm chair on cabriole legs. $160 £80

A lug easy chair, upholstered in crimson and floral tapestry, on oak legs and stretchers. $190 £95

Large early Victorian upholstered arm chair commode on turned legs. $190 £95

Late 19th century lug easy chair on claw and ball feet. $220 £110

Lug easy chair on cabriole legs. $230 £115

A Geoge III mahogany winged easy chair upholstered in floral tapestry and brass studded, standing on cabriole legs with ball and claw feet. $290 £145

A Venetian carved giltwood wing easy chair on cabriole legs. $350 £175

Early 19th century wing chair on square legs with stretchers.
$380 £190

Victorian French style carved giltwood chair upholstered in dark green dralon. $470 £235

George I oak arm chair with panelled back, dated 1723.
$480 £240

Regency tub shaped wing chair with mahogany legs, circa 1820. $490 £245

An early 19th century giltwood arm chair carved in the Louis Quinze manner and upholstered in crushed velvet, on cabriole legs. $600 £300

Early 19th century wing chair upholstered in leather.
$680 £340

Fine George III mahogany saddle wing chair, 81cm. wide. $780 £390

Tub shaped wing chair in Hepplewhite manner, circa 1790. $1,860 £930

George I elm framed wing arm chair, circa 1725.
$2,040 £1,020

119

WING CHAIRS

Queen Anne faded walnut wing chair, circa 1712. $2,550 £1,275

Very fine William and Mary, walnut wing chair. $3,080 £1,540

Queen Anne wing chair with 'C' scroll arms, circa 1705. $3,300 £1,650

George I walnut wing chair with scroll arms. $3,630 £1,815

Late Queen Anne arm chair upholstered in silk damask, 44½in. high. $3,850 £1,925

James II wing chair with elaborately carved scroll work, circa 1685. $3,850 £1,925

George I walnut wing chair, circa 1720. $3,960 £1,980

Queen Anne walnut wing chair with scroll arms and diamond shaped feet. $5,610 £2,805

George III mahogany wing chair with carved paw feet and cabriole legs. $7,700 £3,850

19th century elm
Windsor chair. $18 £9

19th century Windsor
comb back chair. $30 £15

Victorian beechwood
Windsor chair on tur-
ned legs with an 'H'
stretcher. $50 £25

19th century elm
Windsor chair with
a pierced back splat.
            $60 £30

19th century Windsor
comb back arm chair
in elm. $70 £35

Victorian lath back
Windsor chair in
elm. $90 £45

Late 19th century
Windsor child's chair
of ashwood with elm
seat. $110 £55

Ash and elm stick
back Windsor arm
chair, circa 1790.
            $170 £85

Yew wood wheelback
chair, circa 1780.
            $230 £115

WINDSOR CHAIRS

An 18th century comb back Windsor chair with hoof feet. $260 £130

Yew wood Windsor chair with straight legs and crinoline stretcher. $400 £200

Yew wood Windsor chair, circa 1740, with cabriole legs at front. $670 £335

Two of a set of ten Windsor wheelback chairs, circa 1860. $720 £360

Part of a set of eight stick back chairs of golden colour. $1,160 £580

One of a set of five late 18th century yew wood Windsor chairs. $1,270 £635

One of a set of six George III elm Windsor chairs. $1,970 £985

One of a near matching set of six George II yew wood dining chairs. $2,750 £1,375

INDEX